WEIRD & GROSS BIBLE STUFF

WEIRD & GROSS
BIBLE STUFF

WRITTEN BY
RICK **OSBORNE**
ED **STRAUSS**
QUENTIN **GUY**

ILLUSTRATED BY
ANTHONY **CARPENTER**

Zonder**kidz**

Zonder**kidz**.
The children's group of Zondervan
www.zonderkidz.com

Weird & Gross Bible Stuff
Copyright © 2003 by Lightwave Publishing, Inc.
Illustrations Copyright © 2003 by Zondervan

Requests for information should be addressed to:
Grand Rapids, Michigan 49530

ISBN: 0-310-70484-7

Library of Congress Cataloging-in-Publication Data

Osborne, Rick.
 Weird and gross Bible stuff / Rick Osborne.
    p. cm. -- (2:52 soul gear)
Summary: A light-hearted, illustrated look at Bible stories that feature
such things as boils, John eating locusts, and bones coming to life,
plus ideas for how to apply the lessons learned to one's own life.
 ISBN 0-310-70484-7
 1. Bible--Miscellanea--Juvenile literature. [1. Bible--Miscellanea. 2.
Christian life.] I. Title. II. Series.
 BS539.O85 2003
 220.6'1--dc21
                          2003001057

Editor: Gwen Ellis
Art direction and design: Michelle Lenger

Printed in United States
04 05/RRD/5

Contents

GO FIGURE!

The Bible is very funny sometimes. God is the one who invented humor, and he meant for us to laugh. In fact, Proverbs 17:22 says, "A cheerful heart is good medicine." Of course, God didn't make the Bible funny on purpose. It's not a joke book. But certain things that ordinary people do are just plain hilarious, and since the Bible talks about ordinary people, you just know something funny is bound to happen.

Some of the situations that the Bible describes were downright weird. Surprised? Hey, God doesn't think and operate the way we do (See Isaiah 55:8.) And since he's the one calling the shots, you can pretty much expect him to tell people to do strange things sometimes—like asking Isaiah to walk around naked for three years (Isaiah 20:2). Okaaaay.

There are some pretty gross things in the Bible too, such as dogs lapping up their own puke and instructions on how to bury your dung. Like we said, the Bible talks about real people in real-life situations. They weren't so perfect and holy that they never even had to use the bathroom. To the contrary. When one fat king died, his servants didn't open the door to check up on him because they thought that—as usual—he was on the toilet.

Another thing: There's sin in the world and God is in the business of judging evil. That's why proud king Herod was eaten alive by worms, and evil Queen Jezebel was gobbled up by a pack of hungry dogs. We can learn from bad examples too. In fact, we can learn from the silly, funny, and weird stuff in the Bible.

So sit back, start reading, and enjoy yourself—and maybe learn something about God while you do. It'll make you deeper, cooler, smarter, and . . . hey! Who knows? Maybe even stronger! (Luke 2:52)

Tonight's Special Is Thumb-and-Toe Pie

We've all heard of giving scraps of food to the dog under the table. But what if, instead of dogs, you had *kings* under your table? One guy did! Whenever Adoni-Bezek, a Canaanite king, conquered another king, he chopped off that guy's thumbs and big toes and made him beg for scraps under the table (Judges 1:7). Boy, talk about embarrassing! Makes you wonder what the gift shop at Adoni-Bezek's castle was like. Did they have T-shirts that read, "Two thumbs up for Adoni-Bezek"? How about the souvenir stand? "Get your royal toes here!"

Get a Grip—If You Can!

The men of Judah caught Adoni-Bezek (that's Bezek, not *Berserk*), as they were taking over the Promised Land. When they caught him, they chopped off *his* thumbs and big toes (Judges 1:6). A king without thumbs has a really hard time holding on to important things like swords and shields. No grip, no balance, and now he could only count up to sixteen. Adoni-Bezek thought God had paid him back for what he had done to the other kings.

I Didn't Need That Knife Anyway

How fat does a king have to *be* so that when he gets stabbed, his attacker loses the blade in his belly? King Eglon ruled over Israel for 18 years. He was a big, bad tub of jelly and Ehud was the guy who had to "take him out" (Judges 3:16–22). Ehud probably got there, saw Eglon, and thought, *How do you stab a pudding?* Missing a target that big wasn't a concern, though he probably *didn't* expect to lose a foot-and-a-half-long sword! Here's the topper: It's possible that Eglon was in the bathroom when Ehud stabbed him!

THE KING WHO GOT THE POINT

One day a prophet of God told the idol-worshiping king Jeroboam that God was going to bring down his pagan altars. Well, Jeroboam wasn't going to let some religious whackhammer spoil his lovely altars. Jeroboam shouted, "Grab him!" and angrily pointed a pinkie at the prophet. Suddenly, his hand shriveled up like dried fruit, and the altar cracked open and spilled all its ashes (1 Kings 13:4–5). Jeroboam finally learned that it's *not* polite to point.

WHAT DID YOU DO ON YOUR VACATION?

During a seven-day period of time, Zimri killed a king and "wasted" the king's family and friends (1 Kings 16:10–18). That made Zimri the king—for one week. In that week, he committed multiple homicides. Right after that, another king marched toward his palace to capture it. What are you going to do now, Zimri? No answer. Want to know why? Zimri set the palace on fire. And he was *in* the castle when it burned.

DOG PACK LEAVES ROYAL LEFTOVERS

The prophet Elijah told evil Queen Jezebel she was going to die and be gobbled up by dogs—and she was! The dogs left only her skull, hands, and feet (2 Kings 9:34–37). She was such a bad egg that what they ate probably gave them indigestion—*and* bad breath!

A ROYAL TIME-TRAVELER

King Hezekiah lived way back there. Not as far back as the time of the dinosaurs or the creation of the earth or anything like that—but back there. He got really sick—like die sick. When he begged, God let him choose a sign that he would be healed of a sickness. Hezekiah chose for the shadow on a sundial to go backwards (2 Kings 20:8–11). And it *did!* Think about it. How could the sundial go backward unless the sun went backward?

Q: Where does the Jordan River sleep?

A: In its riverbed.

FROM THE PENTHOUSE TO THE DOGHOUSE

King Uzziah thought that he was really hot stuff. He broke the rules and did things that

only priests were allowed to do. That was a no-no in God's book, and suddenly, leprosy broke out on Uzziah's forehead (2 Chronicles 26:18–21). Just like that, Uzziah went from being the "I'll-do-it-*my-way*" king of Judah to Lonely Leper Prince of an Apartment for the rest of his life. It's serious stuff to break God's rules.

KING OF THE PASTURE!

Nebuchadnezzar of Babylon was yet another king who got too big for his britches. In fact, he lost his pants altogether. Nebbie went out of his gourd. His hair grew out like feathers and his fingernails and toenails got all clawy like an eagle's. He lived out in a pasture for seven years and munched grass instead of royal king food (Daniel 4:32–33). Eventually, he regained his grip on reality and returned to his throne, and man, was his attitude improved! "So, God, I'll keep my mouth shut if you promise not to make me eat grass again."

HEROD, THE GREAT BULLY OF BETHLEHEM

King Herod was another royal head-case. "Herod the Great" they called him (he probably told them to call him that). "Herod the Great *Chicken*" was more like it. When he heard about the "King of the Jews" being born in Bethlehem, he gave an order to have all boys two years old and under killed (Matthew 2:16). Oooh! Big man. You're so tough, Herod. Killing little bitty, helpless babies. I mean, are we talking *insecure* or what? But don't worry. Herod soon got *his*. His death was so gross we can't even describe it in this book.

GET COOLER

The kings we have just read about made a royal mess. To get cooler, means avoiding the kind of stupid mistakes they made. Three keys to being a godly leader are:

- Do things God's way.
- Take care of—and care for—the people you lead.
- Don't start thinking God gave you the job because you're his gift to the world and better than every one else. Watch out! God looks for humble men when he's looking for leaders.

HALL OF FAME

HALL OF FAME—KING DAVID

David came rocking on the scene as a kid, then became king and fought enemies endlessly, and then died at a ripe old age. Let's look at a few of the weird and wonderful highlights of his career, beginning with the biggest upset in history—David versus Goliath. Dave was a little shepherd boy, and Goliath was a nine-foot-tall, seasoned warrior. If it sounds like one of the biggest *mis*matches in history, that's because it *was*! But God helped Dave even the odds with one well-slung stone, and that was more than enough to pull off the upset of the eleventh century B.C. (1 Samuel 17:4–51)!

This should have made King Saul happy, but did it? Nuh-uh. He became jealous of David and, next thing you know, he's chasing him all over the countryside, trying to kill him. As he headed for Naioth where David and Samuel were, the Spirit of God hit Saul so hard that he staggered down the road, prophesying. When he found Samuel, Saul (*still* prophesying) stripped, flopped down on the ground, and lay there without his royal robes for a day and a night. David hightailed it out of there (1 Samuel 19:21–24; 20:1). Wouldn't you?

Sometime later, David was going wacko at the gates of Gath. King Saul was still after David and his men, so they split for Philistine-land. (1 Samuel 21:10–15). That was like jumping from the frying pan into the fire, 'cause the Philistines basically said, "*David* is here? David, our worst *enemy*?"

They dragged him in front of the king and David (talk about improvising!) began scratching all over the door like a dog and drooling spit down his beard. The king thought that he was a madman and threw him out. You gotta wonder how David explained how he got out of that predicament.

Many years later, after David was king of Israel, he and his men returned to Gath to fight the rest of the giants living there. These giants were called the sons of Rapha and were feared throughout the region for their tremendous shoe size (35EEE) and their ability to eat fifty-two monster burritos at one sitting. (Now biblical scholars have not proven any of this, but, hey . . . the idea of anything that big and mighty is pretty scary, isn't it?) What we *do* know is that David and his men went up into Giantland (Philistia) and did some serious damage. One particular son of Rapha had six fingers on each hand and six toes on each foot (1 Chronicles 20:6)—probably so he could hold on to his enormous spear and fill up those mondo shoes.

David fought some colossal foes and made some big mistakes, but all in all he was a colossal success—a tremendous king and a man who truly loved God.

A SWEET-TALKING SNAKE

Eve, the first woman, let a snake trick her into disobeying God (Genesis 3). Have you ever thought about how strange that is—a talking snake? Could *all* the animals in the Garden of Eden talk or was it just the serpent? If only the snake talked, shouldn't that have clanged some warning bell in Eve's brain? *Okay, a snake is sweet-talking me. What's wrong with this picture?* But *no,* she just went along with it. Remember this the next time you're at the zoo: If the snake starts talking, one of two things has happened. Either the lemonade's gone bad or your brother is secretly a ventriloquist. Either way, don't answer.

CANNIBAL COWS

Even though his advisers probably told Pharaoh that those late-night anchovy and garlic pizzas would catch up with him, he apparently didn't listen. (Not listening seemed to be something most kings were good at.) So he ended up with this crazy dream about seven fat, happy cows being eaten by seven skinny, mean cows (Genesis 41:1–4). Weird! Fortunately, God told Joseph what the dream meant—seven years of plenty to

be followed by seven years of famine in Egypt. Pharaoh probably was a little freaked out after that dream. It probably wouldn't have gone well for anyone who jumped out from hiding and yelled "Moo!"

FLIES AND GNATS DRIVE A WHOLE NATION CRAZY

Don't flies drive you nuts? One little, teeny-tiny fly buzz-buzzing around your food and suddenly you're Rambo, cyborg-mercenary fly-killer, jumping on the furniture and hanging from the ceiling fan with a rolled-up magazine in your fist. It could be worse. You could have been back in ancient Egypt when God sent bijillions of flies and gnats because Pharaoh wouldn't straighten up and fly right (Exodus 8:16–24). Needless to say, the Egyptians were supremely annoyed *and* they didn't have any magazines to roll up. They wrote on bricks. "Hold still! I'll get the one on your head!"

An Army of Hornets

When Joshua and his men were ready to conquer the land of Canaan, God sent hornets ahead of them to conquer Canaan (Joshua 24:12). God didn't want Joshua or his men taking credit for the victory, so God set up a "sting operation" and sent some bugs to do a man's job.

Lions Lunch on New Neighbors

When the Israelites were sent into exile because of their sin, the Samaritans moved into their old neighborhood. The first thing they did was to start worshiping their idols. ROAR! Suddenly, there were lions everywhere, eating people up (2 Kings 17:26). The Bible says that God sent the lions because the new settlers didn't know what God required them to do. This was *not* an ideal welcome to the suburbs of Samaria.

Fire-Breathing Swamp Dragon

God told Job about an enormous creature called Leviathan. You really wanna hope that this was all *symbolic,* 'cause if there *is* some gigantic fire-breathing reptile out there in the swamps, it makes you kind of want to cancel your fishing trip to the Everglades, huh? Take a look in your Bible (Job 41) to learn more about this fearsome creature.

CREATURES WITH FOUR FACES

In a vision, Ezekiel saw four living creatures, and each one had four faces. Each of the four had four faces. One was the face of a lion, another an ox, a third a man, and the last an eagle (Ezekiel 1:5–10; see also Revelation 4). That was a scary vision.

THE FOUR-HEADED, FOUR-WINGED LEOPARD

God gave Daniel visions of the strangest zoo in the galaxy. Only a prophet could claim to have seen a four-headed leopard with wings and not get locked up some-where! (Daniel 7:6). The leopard symbolized ancient Greece under Alexander the Great— powerful and fast. The vision also showed how Alexander's empire would break apart into four separate kingdoms after his death–that's the four heads. After reading about these

Q: Why didn't Moses take any howler monkeys on the ark?

A: Moses didn't go on the ark.

creatures, going to your local zoo will seem boring. "Hey, son, check out the leopard." "He's okay, Dad, but he only has one head and no wings." "You been reading Daniel again, boy?"

THE UNICORN GOAT

If you thought a four-headed, winged leopard is strange, check out the one-horned speed-goat in Daniel 8:5—*another* vision. *There's* something you don't see every day! Again, it wasn't real. It symbolized something. But God's visions and special effects are great!

SEA CRUISE INSIDE A FISH'S GUTS

So, you know all about Jonah—he ran from God, got swallowed by a big fish (Jonah 1:17), and then, *finally*, did what God wanted him to do. What do you think it was like to actually *be* in the fish's belly? "Nasty" wouldn't begin to describe it! Imagine the smell inside there—partially

digested fish, old banana peels, and rancid, sticky saliva. Yuck! And don't forget the stomach acids! They would burn your hair off in patches, bleach your skin to a pale white, dissolve most of your clothes . . . *what fun*! But you can bet that when God had the fish barf Jonah up on the beach, he definitely got people's attention!

As if the whole fish episode weren't bad enough, Jonah got all worked up over a shady vine. God made the vine, then sent a worm to eat the roots. Scrub one vine. Jonah was so steamed that he wanted to die right there (Jonah 4:7–8)! Easy, man.
At least this time the worm didn't swallow *you*.

THE WOMAN IN A FLYING STORK BASKET

The prophet Zechariah had a strange—*very* strange— vision, this time about the rebellious people of Judah being taken to Babylon (Zechariah 5:5–11). A woman named "Wickedness" is stuffed down into a basket (like a laundry basket), then some stork women come along, grab the basket, and fly it off to Babylon.

Q:
What's the moral of the story of Jonah and the great fish?

A: You just can't keep a good man down.

DEMONIC PIGS STAMPEDE OFF CLIFF

Jesus cast a whole mess of demons out of one very crazy guy. The demons weren't too excited about going back to hell, so they left the crazy guy and swarmed into a herd of pigs (Luke 8:27–33). The swine apparently weren't too happy about being invaded, and they did the lemming-leap off a cliff. The crazy guy got his brain back, the pigs found out they couldn't swim, and the high-diving demons got sent back to you know where.

PETER AT THE CRAWLY CRITTER BUFFET

God threw Peter for a loop with a little test about his eating habits (Acts 10:9–15). "Hey, Pete." "Yes, Lord?" "Remember all those things that Moses told you not to eat because you're Jewish?" "Of course, Lord." "Well, eat them. Eat lizards, bugs, shellfish, snakes, maybe a vulture or two." Fortunately for Peter, there were no brussels sprouts and because it was only a vision that disappeared, he never had to chew.

LOCUST-HORSES WITH SCORPION TAILS

Welcome to the Revelation Exhibit of Wacky and Alarming End-Time Creatures! You see, John had a vision about the end of the world while he was on the island of Patmos—and *what* a vision! Here you have a sort of locust-horse mix with a rather sharp-toothed human face and a scorpion's tail (Read it in Revelation 9:7–11). They were so ugly, they were hideous, and they had an attitude to match. Let's call 'em "Abaddon's Bad Boys" after their king, the angel of the Abyss. No, you can't have one, even if you promise to feed it and keep it on heavy tranquilizers.

LION-HEADED HORSES WITH SNAKEHEAD TAILS

Moving right along in John's end-time vision, we come to *these* unique monsters. They look like horses with lion-like heads and tails that look like snakes (Revelation 9:17–19). They were spewing clouds of fire, sulfur, and smoke from their mouths. They could get you coming *and* going! (At this

Q: When Aaron threw Moses' rod on the ground, it became a snake. What would it have become if he'd thrown it into the Nile?

A: Wet.

time, please put on your gas masks.) It's worse than that old neighborhood dog with bad breath.

THE SEVEN-HEADED BEAST

There seems to be no shortage of terrifying creatures in John's visions. Here's a little scarlet number with seven heads and ten horns (Revelation 12:3)—and yes, guys, he's *really* nasty.

GET SMARTER

God made everything, including all the marvelous creatures here on earth and all the amazing beings and creatures in heaven. God is very creative and imaginative. And want to know something? We are like God when we come up with new ideas, draw imaginative drawings, and write fantastic stories. But remember, God is good and righteous and his character guides all his creative efforts. When you use your imagination, be sure that you are using it to promote what is godly and good.

Q: Which baseball team in the Bible was so good that even their very worst batter hit ten home runs?

A: The children of Israel in the desert. "No one gathered less than ten homers." (Numbers 11:32)

Q. Who was the greatest comedian in the Bible?

A. Samson. He brought the house down.

Q: Why was Moses buried in the land of Moab?

A: He was dead.

Q: Was there any money on Noah's ark?

A: Yes, the duck had a bill and the frog had a greenback.

Q: What was the difference between the thirty-two thousand soldiers Gideon started with and the three hundred he had left?

A: 31,700 soldiers.

Q: How do we know that Abraham was almost as wise as Solomon?

A: Because he knew a Lot.

A Staircase to Heaven

Once Jacob was on a journey and had to sleep by the side of the road. He couldn't avoid it. So he found a rock and used it for a pillow. That night he dreamed about a stairway to heaven with angels walking up and coming down. When Jacob woke up, he thought he'd discovered a secret portal into heaven, so he marked the spot by pouring oil on his rock pillow (Genesis 28:10–18).

The Donkey That Talked Back

God sent an angel to stop Balaam from going where he shouldn't go. Balaam couldn't see the angel, but his donkey could. Balaam started yelling at his donkey. He even beat her. Still the donkey wouldn't move. Finally the donkey just spoke out and told him off (Numbers 22:21–33). Ho! You know you're pretty bad-off when your *donkey* has to clue you in.

The Bird Man of Brook Cherith

Ravens brought Elijah bread and meat twice a day while the prophet hung out and waited for God's command in the wilderness (1 Kings 17:2–6). Probably history's first recorded fast-food delivery. But Elijah probably didn't have to tip the ravens.

DEATH GETS THE DAY OFF—TWICE!

You're born, you live, and then you die, right? But hold the phone! There were two guys we know of who actually *didn't* die, Enoch and Elijah. Nope, God just skipped the kick-the-bucket routine with them. Enoch "walked with God; then he was no more because God took him away" (Genesis 5:24), and Elijah went out twister-style, riding a whirlwind to heaven (2 Kings 2).

FIRST-ROUND KNOCKOUT

God's enemies kept playing "Our gods are bigger than your God." (*No way* they could win this one, but they tried.) The Philistines captured the ark of the covenant. "Whoo-hoo! We're number one!" They put it in the temple of their fish god, Dagon. The next morning, Dagon was lying facedown in front of the ark (1 Samuel 5:1–4)! You can see the priests trying to figure *that* one out! "Hmm, yeah, he must've slipped. Must be the new floor polish." Poor little fish-god priests!

GOLDEN RATS, GOLDEN TUMORS

When the Philistines stole the ark of the covenant, God sent them a painful plague, complete with tumors. Youch! The Philistines were not only anxious to return the ark, but they sent some gifts back with it. Can't you see the Israelites asking, "What's *this*?" Golden knickknacks, tumors, and rats? The Philistines had sent little gold statues of rats and tumors as a way of saying, "Please take the ark home" (1 Samuel 5:6–12; 6:4–5, 11).

SPECIAL SOUND EFFECTS!

The huge army of Arameans that was camped around Jerusalem ran away because God made them hear the sound of a mighty army descending on them (2 Kings 7:6–7)! How do you think God *did* this? Remember, this was before special effects, canned sound, and surround-sound. Maybe God used a lot of angels banging coconuts. It doesn't really matter *how* it happened; it matters that God *can help us* when we're in deep trouble.

A HAND-DELIVERED MESSAGE

King Belshazzar, a Babylonian king, was living large, pagan style. He was throwing a party for all of his rich friends and dishonoring God by drinking wine from the sacred bowls stolen from God's temple in Jerusalem. You just *know* something's gonna happen! Sure enough, a mysterious floating hand—*just* a hand, no body, mind you—appears from nowhere and writes a message of doom on the wall (Daniel 5:5). God shut the Babylonians down that very night. You gotta hand it to God! He sure knows how to deliver a message!

DRY BONES MARCHING

Ezekiel had a vision of dry old bones coming back to life. Imagine you're Ezekiel, standing in a valley full of old bones. At God's command, you tell them to live. A huge rattle shakes the air. Bones rise up and join into skeletons. (Sounds like a bad costume-party experience, where everyone came in the same costume.) Suddenly you see them get muscles, then tendons, and then skin. (Try having a good night's sleep after seeing *this!*) Then wind rushes into the valley and, with a great whooshing breath, an army comes to life (Ezekiel 37:1–10).

WORDS OF POWER

Jesus needed only three words to knock over a group of priests and soldiers: "I am he" (John 18:5). At these three little words they "drew back and fell to the ground." Wow! No wonder he told Peter to put his sword away (John 18:6–11). I don't think he *needed* it.

NOON OF THE LIVING DEAD

Some pretty strange things happened the day of Jesus' crucifixion: darkness at noon, the tearing of the temple veil, an earthquake, and then *this* one—dead people rising from the grave and walking the streets (Matthew 27:52–53). Can you imagine anything more weird? Perhaps their friends and relatives said, "We thought you were dead. We gave your room to Uncle Micah."

TRUE GRIT

Paul had a job to do and he wasn't going to die until it was done. Here's his own list of the times that others tried to send him to heaven early: "Five times I received . . . forty lashes minus one. Three times I was beaten with rods, once I was stoned, three times I was ship-wrecked, I spent a night and a day in the open sea . . . I have been in danger from rivers, in danger from bandits, in danger . . . in danger . . . in danger . . . in danger . . . in danger . . . *and* in danger" (2 Corinthians 11:21–33). And *we* think we're suffering if we don't get a good seat at church or if the sermon's too long.

GET DEEPER

What is normal? We think that certain things are weird if they are different from what we are used to. We can usually only do things a couple different ways. But God is supernatural and can do anything he wants, any way he wants, any *time* he wants. We shouldn't think it's weird if God does things in a supernatural way or answers our prayers in a way we never expected him to. Sometimes he gives us "more than all we ask or imagine" (Ephesians 3:20). Tell God what you want. Then let him surprise you with the way he answers.

WEIRD TRIVIA

Q: The prophet Isaiah walked around naked for three years. True or false?

A: True. (Isaiah 20:3)

Q: A disciple of Jesus ran away naked through some olive trees to avoid being arrested. True or false?

A: True. (Mark 14:51–52)

Q: Absalom was riding his donkey through the woods when the donkey saw an angel and refused to go any farther. True or false?

A: False. Balaam's donkey was the one who saw an angel. (Numbers 22:21–23)

Q: A group of new Christians lit a bon fire and burned their old books of magic spells. True or false?

A: True. (Acts 19:19)

Q: When Peter saw a sheet full of animals, God told him, "Get up, Peter. Kill and eat."

A: False. It was only a *vision.* (Acts 10:9–16)

Q: Some people thought Paul and Barnabas were the Greek gods Zeus and Hermes. True or false?

A: True. (Acts 14:11-13)

Q: For six days of the week, if the Israelites tried to keep some manna overnight, it became full of maggots and began to stink. However, on Friday night they could store some. True or false?

A: True. (Exodus 16:19-24)

Q: The Law of Moses said the Israelites were *not* allowed to eat the beak and the feet of birds. True or false?

A: False. They were only told not to eat the blood. (Leviticus 7:26)

Q: The Israelites used the hides of sea cows to cover the altar of the tabernacle. True or false?

A: True. (Numbers 4:11)

Q: God sent giant hailstones down to part the Red Sea. True or false?

A: False. He used a strong wind to part the sea. (Exodus 14:21)

ANGEL STUFF

HEADS UP! INSPECTION TIME!

A crazy mob of messed-up people tried to get Lot to turn over his two guests to them—which was a *baaaad* idea. Lot's guests were angels who had been sent as inspectors to see how wicked the city was. Surprise! The citizens of Sodom failed the inspection. (I mean, like *really* failed.) After Lot and his family left, the sky rained fire and burning sulphur on Sodom and its sister city, Gomorrah. Both were reduced to nothing (Genesis 19:4–25).

IN THIS CORNER, JACOB! IN THE OTHER . . .

When Jacob wrestled with the Angel of God all night long, he earned a new name, "Israel" (meaning "he struggles with God"). (Genesis 32:24–28.) You gotta give Jake credit for hanging in there, even after his opponent pulled a move that most modern-day wrestlers would love to know—the ol' dislocate-the-hip-with-one-touch move! That slowed Jacob down, but he still hung on until he got God's blessing. That's a prize worth fighting for. Who wants a reeally ugly, oversized wrestling belt?

CROWD OF MILLIONS EATS ANGELS' FOOD

Imagine eating the same thing every meal, every day, year after year for forty years. The Israelites did just that when they ate manna, something that tasted like honey-flavored wafers. It appeared each morning in the desert (Exodus 16:14) and was later called "angel food" (Psalm 78:25). After forty years, even angel food didn't taste so great.

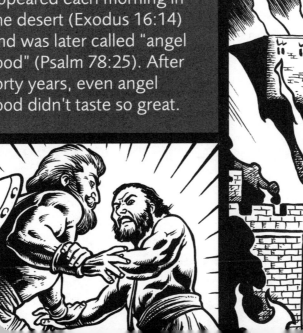

BARBECUE, ANGEL STYLE

An angel (Gideon thought it was a man) told Gideon that God would help him defeat Israel's enemies. Gideon wasn't convinced but asked the angel if he wanted to stay for lunch. When he brought out the meat

and bread, the angel touched the food with his staff and— presto—flame shot up and all the food was *gone!* Then the angel vanished (Judges 6:11–22). Gideon was left hungry but convinced.

AN ANGEL COOKS A PROPHET'S LUNCH

One time Elijah was hiding out in the wilderness feeling sorry for himself, so God sent an angel chef to make him a few meals. It was some serious power chow. You could make a fortune selling this stuff to backpackers! It kept Elijah going for the next forty days and nights! (1 Kings 19:3–8).

ONE-ANGEL WRECKING CREW

The Assyrian army insulted God and surrounded Jerusalem. God sent an angel into the Assyrian camp to wipe out 185,000 soldiers (2 Kings 19:35). Yes, *one* angel against 185,000. Needless to say, the king of Assyria grabbed the remains of his army and hightailed it out of there. God's got more power in his little finger (so to speak) than all the armies in the history of mankind.

MICHAEL VERSUS THE PRINCE OF PERSIA

God sent one of his archangels, Michael, to help Gabriel get a message through to Daniel. We're talking some serious enemy interference on the spiritual level because it took Gabriel three *weeks* to get through. Now, God's angels are not usually as slow as the postal service. They're usually quicker than instant messaging e-mail. But Gabriel had to duke it out with some demon called

Q: How do angels greet each other?

A: They wave halo.

the "Prince of Persia" (Daniel 10:13). We know it's a demon because if the "prince" had been a human being, he would've lasted about two seconds with an angel.

NOTE TO SELF: DON'T TALK BACK TO ANGELS

John the Baptist's parents were old when he was born, so when an angel came and told John's dad, Zechariah, that his wife was going to have a baby, Zechariah basically said, "Yeah, right." The angel said, "Look, pal, I'm Gabriel. I stand in God's presence and relay the words from his mouth to your ears. You want a sign? How about this? You don't get to speak until the baby's born. How do you like them apples?" (Luke 1:11–20). (An angel wouldn't say "them apples." Or "pal" either, probably. But you get the idea.)

MICHAEL BOOTS THE DRAGON OUT OF HEAVEN

Some people think God and Satan are equal and opposite powers. Not a chance! It's more like Godzilla versus Barney! No twelve-round battle here—it's stomp! squish! and goodnight purple puppet! When Satan got kicked out of heaven for rebelling against God, it's not like God said, "Oh, no! Lucifer is too strong—I'll have to fight him myself!" It was more like, "Michael?" "Yes, Lord?" And then God's *angels* kicked the dragon out (Revelation 12:7–9).

GET DEEPER

The Bible says that God's angels are "ministering spirits sent to serve those who will inherit salvation" (Hebrews 1:14). Meaning, they're sent to serve Christians. We're not really sure of *all* that angels do or how they do it, but after reading some of the stuff about them, it's good to know they're on *our* side! They're helping out in ways and at times that we don't even know about. When we arrive in heaven, we'll get to hang out with the angels and hear their stories firsthand.

HALL OF FAME—SAMSON

Sure, John Henry was strong, but he never *existed!* Samson, son of Zanoah, was the real deal, the genuine Man of Steel. This guy ripped two-ton city gates out of their sockets, single-handedly wiped out entire armies, shredded lions, and snapped thick ropes like so much spaghetti. Here are some highlights from his astonishing life.

Samson was either as cool as a cucumber or as dumb as an acorn. When a lion attacked him, he was cool. The Spirit of God gave Samson the strength to tear it apart. Pretty impressive, huh? When Samson saw the lion again, a swarm of bees had built a hive in the lion's carcass (Judges 14:5–9). Samson's mom probably had told him not to eat food out of dead animals, but did Samson pay any attention? Nope. He just walks up, "Oh, look," he says, "the golden carcass fast food!" and grabs himself a big ol' handful of honey.

As strong as he was, Samson thought he was an even better prankster, so he came up with a riddle to trick some Philistine hotshots (Judges 14:14–18). "Out of the eater, something to eat; out of the strong, something sweet." Probably took him hours. When they convinced his wife to tell them the answer, he came up with an even better line: "If you had not plowed with my heifer, you would not have solved my riddle." *Heifer?* That's, like, a cow! Something says their marriage wasn't destined for greatness.

Samson's amazing strength made him someone you *really* didn't want to cross. But the Philistines did. So not only does Samson catch three hundred foxes, he ties their tails together in pairs, sets a torch between each pair of tails, and then turns them loose on the Philistines' crops (Judges 15:4–5). The fur was flying with fiery foxes. The Philistines lose, the foxes definitely lose, and Samson says, "*What?* You started it!"

In one episode, we see the strong man ripping the Gaza city gates right off the hinges and putting them on a nearby hilltop (Judges 16:3). Not that the men of Gaza didn't deserve to lose their gates, but can you imagine the conversation that led up to this? "Little Philistines, little Philistines, I'm Samson. Open your gates." "Not by the beards on our chinny-chin-chins." "Then I'll huff and I'll puff and I'll rip your doors off."

In another episode of Samson the Philistine Exterminator . . .
... the big guy takes on a whole army with a bone. Yes, friends, a thousand of Philistia's finest brought low by a muscle-bound man of God swinging a donkey's jaw

(Judges 15:15–17). Can you imagine the sports commentary on this? "Hundreds are down, and yet—they're *still* coming!" And can you imagine the last two Philistines after 998 have been killed? "I know he's killed everyone else, but I think the two of us can take him!" Yeah, *riiight!* (Judges 16:4–21).

Samson had the ultimate "bad hair day." When Delilah asks him what the secret of his strength is, Samson says, "Tie me up with seven leather straps, and I'll become weak." Samson snoozes, Delilah ties him up, but he wakes up and snaps the straps. She bugs him again, so he says, "Tie me with ropes." Soon as he's snoozing she ties him with ropes. Samson wakes up, snaps the ropes. She bugs him again. He says, "Tie up my hair." He falls asleep, she ties up his hair. He wakes up and snaps the tie. *Finally* she nags him for days and finally dumb, dumb Samson says, "Okay, okay. Just cut my hair" (Judges 16:15–21). Like, *duh*! Didn't he think she would cut his hair?

After Samson lost his locks, he lost his strength and was locked in prison. The Philistines never clued in that when his hair grew back, his strength might return. One day they brought him out with a plan to mock him. Samson shoved the stone temple pillars apart and brought down the roof. Three thousand Phillistines died.

BIZARRE HEALINGS

ANTIDOTE FOR SNAKEBITE

Once, when the Israelites were whining and bad-mouthing God, a whole slew of venomous snakes slithered into camp to take a bite. When the Israelites caught sight of the wriggling horde, they realized that they needed an attitude change and cried out to God for help. God told Moses to make a bronze serpent and put it on a pole. If those who had been bitten looked at the snake-on-a-stick they would be miraculously healed. It was *way* better than the cut-and-suck-the-venom-out method (Numbers 21:4–9).

THE SPIT-IN-THE-DIRT-AND-HEAL-THE-EYES-WITH-MUD CURE

Jesus goes up to a blind man, spits in the dirt, and puts some of the mud on the man's eyes. When the man washes it off, he can see (John 9:6–7)! Jesus never did this again. He never went with the same method twice, probably because people would have started thinking it was some religious ritual that they, too, could perform to heal people. Nuh-uh. Not how it works. ("Dude, get that mud out of my eyes! That's nasty!" "But *Jesus* did it that way!" "Two things: One, you ain't Jesus. And two, I'm not blind. I just stubbed my toe.")

BOY'S MOM DECIDES NOT TO BURY HIM

Under the heading of "In the Nick of Time," Jesus brought a widow's dead son back to life while they were carrying his body out to bury him. You could say he was a real mummy's boy (Luke 7:11–15).

FOUR DAYS AND STINKY, STINKY, STINKY

By the time Jesus arrived at the scene, Lazarus had been in the tomb for four days. "Lord, what *took* you so long?" Jesus then told them to take away the stone from the front of Lazarus's tomb. His sister Martha said, "But Lord, he's been in there for four days. He'll *stink!*" They rolled the stone door to the tomb away anyway, and Jesus raised Lazarus from the dead. (Martha probably didn't give him a hug until after he'd had a *couple* of baths (John 11:17–44).

Q: How many New Testament books are named after James?

A: Seven. All the rest of them are named *before* James.

PETER'S SHADOW HEALS SICK PEOPLE

God's power is so incredible that even Peter's shadow healed the sick when it touched them (Acts 5:15)! And no, this isn't Peter *Pan* we're talking about—although it would have been cool if Peter could have gone one way on his mission to help people, and his shadow could have gone another way. He would have gotten twice the work done!

PAUL'S LAUNDRY HEALS THE SICK

Paul's ministry was totally rockin'—people were using pieces of clothing that had touched him to heal the sick (Acts 19:12)! Can you imagine? "And the latest from Asia Minor: Paul of Tarsus's gym locker was raided in a health club in Ephesus. Paul reported missing a towel, some socks, and a sweaty handkerchief."

GET STRONGER

We should pray that God will help us stay healthy. He made our bodies and knows how they work. But we should also pray that God would give us the self-discipline and wisdom that we need to eat properly, exercise, sleep well, stay clean, and generally take care of our bodies. God's power can heal us, but we should never take our bodies or our health for granted. They're great gifts from God, and we need to look after them.

Q: Why didn't Noah go fishing?

A: He only had two worms!

Q: Why couldn't anyone on the ark play cards?

A: Because Noah was standing on the deck.

Q: Who was the greatest sinner in the Bible?

A: Moses. He broke all the Ten Commandments at once. (Exodus 32:19)

Q: Jacob's son Gad named two of his sons Arodi and Areli. True or false?

A: True. (Genesis 46:16)

Q: Jacob's son Benjamin named two of his sons Muppim and Huppim.
True or false?

A: True. (Genesis 46:21)

Q: Jacob's son Simeon named two of his sons Chazir and Challah. True or false?

A: False. Chazir means pig and Challah means cake. Who would give their kids names like *that?*

Q: Methuselah was the oldest man in the Bible. He lived 969 years. How then did he die before his father?

A: Because his father, Enoch, never died. He was taken up to heaven.

Q: Why did Absalom's Pillar stand in the King's Valley near Jerusalem?
A: It would have looked dumb lying on the ground.

Q: Did Noah really have great big lights attached to the top of the ark?
A: Oh, yeah. They were floodlights.

Q: What is Puah famous for? (Genesis 46:13)
A: He was the Israelite who found Christopher Robin in Hundred Acre Woods.

Q: Did the prophet Jeremiah have a horse?
A: Yup. His name was "Iz Me." Jeremiah was always saying, "Woe iz me!"

Q: How many days did Jonadab spend in the belly of the great fish?

A: None. But *Jonah* was there for three days.

I Said, " 'Talk' to the Rock!"

The Israelites were whining again. "We're thirrrr-ssty! We want waaa-terrrr! Wahhh!" Moses goes to God. God says to talk to the rock to get some water, but by this time Moses is so steamed at the whiners that he smacks the rock with his staff—*twice* (Numbers 20:7–12). Oops! Yeah, God brought water out of the rock, but God had to have a chat with Moses afterward. (It's a good thing God hadn't told Moses to ask some *person* for water.)

Today's Forecast: Lots (and Lots!) of Sun, with Occasional Hailstones

Joshua asked God for enough time to defeat the Amorites, and God gave it to him by stopping the sun in mid-sky for almost a full day! That was one short day for Israel and one looooong day for the Amorites—especially since God not only sent extra sunshine but threw in a bonus of gigantic hailstones to pummel the Amorites (Joshua 10:10–14).

THE FOOD THAT NEVER RAN OUT

Elijah's longest *ongoing* miracle was when God made a widow's food supply last for years (1 Kings 17:12–16). When she met Elijah, she only had enough left for *one* meal, but she shared it with Elijah, and God made that one meal's worth of food last three-and-a-half years. Now *that's* stretching your grocery budget!

GOD'S ALL-CONSUMING FIRE

Elijah took on Baal's prophets
to prove who was following the
real God (1 Kings 18:20–40). The
God that burned up the sacrifice was the *true* God. After
Baal's boys bombed out, Elijah was so confident that God
would win, he soaked his sacrifice with water three times,
then prayed that God would answer. Fire rushed down from
heaven, burning up the sacrifice, the wood, the stones, the
dirt, and the water around them. "Yahweh! Yahweh! He is
God! Baal's boys are dumb as sod!"

CAN WE TRY THIS AGAIN?

The idolatrous king of Samaria sent a captain with fifty soldiers to arrest Elijah. The captain demanded that Elijah come
down the hill. Now! *Fwoosh!* Fire fell from heaven and it was
scorch city for them. Another captain came with fifty more

men. He too ordered Elijah down the hill. What was he *thinking*? Again, *fwoosh!* The third captain must've been clued in, because he approached the hill with a lot of knee-knocking and tooth-chattering. Stumbling between the burned sandals and helmets, he fell on his knees and begged for their lives (2 Kings 1:9–14).

FEEDING THE MASSES

One time Jesus fed a crowd of four thousand men (not including women and children) using one kid's lunch—a few fishes and loaves of bread (John 6:1–11). Bigger crowds started following him after this. It's no wonder! Can you imagine if you could do this? Buy one chili dog at a baseball game and keep handing it out till everyone is fed. Of course, everyone, stuffed full of chili dogs, in a crowded stadium probably is not such a good idea. But the bread and fish meal was a great idea. It worked for the hungry crowd Jesus fed.

Q: Was Zacchaeus a prophet during the days of Jeremiah of Isaiah?

A: Neither. He was a tax collector in Jesus' day.

WALKING ON WATER

The disciples are out on a lake (in a boat, of course) when they see Jesus walking toward them. *On the water!* Naturally, they freak out. Except for Peter. He says, "Hey, *I* wanna do that!" Now, this is no calm fishpond. We're talking storm-tossed waves miles from land. Peter walks out a ways, then thinks, "I must be out of my mind!" Bloop! Down he goes (Matthew 14:22–33). Jesus pulls him out, stands him on the surface again like some half-drowned cat, then walks him back to the boat.

A SORCERER STRUCK BLIND

The sorcerer Elymas was lying to the governor of Cyprus, filling his head with garbage, but when Barnabas and Paul showed up with the Gospel, the Holy Spirit gave Paul the scoop on the sad-sack sorcerer. Paul said, "God sees you, devil-boy. Lights out for now." (Okay, he didn't say that, but that's what he meant.) Elymas went blind (Acts 13:6–11) and had to be led out by the hand before he stumbled over any expensive vases.

GET DEEPER

We often run up against obstacles and problems, things that get in our way or make going forward difficult. Problems can make daily life a pain. Sometimes we think there are too many obstacles to get over or that a problem is just too big to solve, but the Bible says that with God all things are possible (Matthew 19:26). Pray and trust him. He'll either give you wisdom to go through problems, move them out of the way, or make them disappear.

 # REMARKABLE MIRACLES

Two-for-one special—Aaron had one of those miracle staffs that God liked his early prophets to use. Aaron's turned into a snake, then it ate the two snake staffs belonging to Pharaoh's magicians (Exodus 7:8–12).

The leaders of the twelve tribes of Israel all thought that if they had a staff that looked like Aaron's, then they could be in charge too—only, when all the staffs were collected, only Aaron's budded, bloomed, and produced almonds (Numbers 17:8)!

Gideon kept asking God for signs—first, that God would wet a wool fleece with dew and keep the ground around it dry; then, after God did that, he asked him to make the ground wet and keep the fleece dry (Judges 6:36–40). Done and done! Next?

God told Elijah to wait for him at Mount Horeb. As Elijah waited, a powerful wind blew by, an earthquake rumbled and fire roared, but God wasn't in any of them. In a beautiful, quiet miracle, God came in a still, soft whisper after the fire (1 Kings 19:11–13).

Spiffy prophet wardrobe—a cloak that you roll up, strike rivers with, and they part in the middle so you can walk across on dry land (2 Kings 2:8). Of course, you have to be a prophet for this to work.

Elisha had the Israelites dig ditches all through a dry desert valley, prophesying that the ditches would be filled with water the next morning—and sure enough, they were (2 Kings 3:16–20).

Elisha did his own version of feeding a multitude, when God helped him make twenty loaves of bread feed a group of one hundred hungry soldiers (2 Kings 4:42–44).

News flash! After an iron ax-head sank to the bottom of the Jordan River, a prophet with incredible faith made it rise and float on the water's surface (2 Kings 6:5–7).

The prophet Elisha was so in tune that God could speak to him and repeat the military plans that the king of Aram talked about in his bedroom! (2 Kings 6:8–12).

The power of words! Jesus performed many healings simply by speaking. He said, "Be clean!" to a centurion with a sick servant (Matthew 8:13).

Jesus was so cool! One day he took a nap on a boat during a wild storm at sea, and his friends were all freaking out, thinking they were going to drown. Jesus gets up, stretches, and tells the storm to chill out. And it did! (Matthew 8:23–26).

A woman was healed merely by touching the edge of Jesus' cloak (Matthew 9:20–22). In fact, whole *crowds* of sick people did the same thing and were healed (Matthew 14:35–36).

Take *that*, taxman! Jesus had Peter go catch a fish, telling him that he would find a four-drachma coin in its mouth to pay their taxes. First fish Peter snagged, sure enough, there was the coin, worth four drachmas (Matthew 17:24–27). (Now *why* do you suppose a fish tried to swallow a coin in the first place?)

Peter was a fisherman by trade, so when Jesus told him to try again after he'd been at fishing all night, he was thinking, *Come on!* But he changed his mind when Jesus provided a catch so big that their nets started to break! (Luke 5:4–7).

LEAVE IT ALONE! IT'LL SCAR!

Practically overnight, Job lost everything—his livestock, his servants, and then his kids. To top it all off, his entire body broke out in painful, ugly, disgusting boils. He sat down behind the house where oven ashes were dumped and scraped those sores with broken pottery pieces. Apparently they were infected and painful (Job 2:7–8; 7:15).

THIRSTY FOR BLOOD, ANYONE?

Moses put his staff in the great Nile River and turned the river to blood. The fish died, bloated, and floated on top of the bloody river, and the air filled with flies and stench. Looking at tap water under the microscope back then would have been *very* interesting. But *still* Pharaoh didn't let God's people go (Exodus 7:14–24). Stubbornness is thicker than blood, it seems.

ROTTING HEAPS OF FROG CORPSES

If the Egyptians thought their *river* stank, what were they thinking when the plague of *frogs* hit? Frogs everywhere was crazy enough, but when they died, they didn't just magically disappear to make way for the next plague—there were so many there was nowhere to put them all. They stacked these rotting green hoppers in heaps (Exodus 8:1–15). The stink was so bad the Egyptians probably were the first people in history to put clothespins on their noses.

WHAT GOES AROUND COMES AROUND

Everybody loves babies, right? They're warm, soft, and cuddly. Who could imagine ever hurt-

ing one? Try Pharaoh. He got all freaked out that the Hebrews were having lots of kids—enough to maybe rebel against him when they grew up. His "solution"? He ordered the Hebrews to throw all their newborn boys into the Nile River (Exodus 1:16, 22). It doesn't get a lot worse than that. Well, you reap what you sow, and eighty years later, when God sent the ten plagues on Egypt, guess what died in the last one? All the firstborn sons of *Egypt!* (Exodus 11:4–5).

THE MAN WITH ONE THOUSAND WIVES

Solomon was supposed to be the wisest man in the world—at least God made him that way, originally. Later, Solomon forgot God and did what he wanted to do, which led to remarkable *non*-wisdom. An obvious example is that he married seven hundred women and had three hundred concubines (1 Kings 11:3). What part of Solomon's brain thought *that* would be a good idea? It takes a lot of work and prayer to keep *one* good marriage going, but one *thou-sand*? Forget it!

VOMIT VERSES

Every time the Bible talks about vomiting, it describes how sin makes you sick. Sin messes with people's spiritual innards the same way a chocolate-liver-spinach milkshake churns up your guts. There's so much vomit in the following verses that you almost need hip waders as you read them.

A drunkard staggers around in his vomit."
(Isaiah 19:14)

All the tables are covered with vomit."
(Isaiah 28:8)

"Get drunk and vomit, and fall to rise no more."
(Jeremiah 25:27)

"Let Moab wallow in her vomit."
(Jeremiah 48:26)

Burning Dead Men's Bones

King Josiah destroyed the pagan altar at Bethel (cool), killed the pagan priests (this is getting *rough*), then began digging up human skeletons and burning them on the altar. Whoa! Stink! What's Josiah *doing*? Relax. He's just following orders. Hundreds of years earlier, a prophet of God said that since the people were evil to the bone, they would meet their match in a bone-burning king (1 Kings 13:1–2, 32; 2 Kings 23:15–16, 20).

Lunch At The Pigpen Buffet

Jesus told the story of a young man who blew his inheritance on partying and girls. He ended up in a pigpen, mud-wrestling the pigs for a few husks to eat before he finally decided to go home. When he did, his dad forgave him (Luke 15:11–24). Sounds warm and cuddly, huh? But

first picture this: Kid shows up dressed in rags, covered in mud, smelling high as a hog (*Pheeeweee!*) OK, *now* picture daddy running up and throwing his arms around him for one of them big ol' hugs. *That* is love!

GET COOLER

All we have to do to see things that are gross is turn on the news or watch the latest "thriller" out of Hollywood. Even life itself contains things that are unavoidably gross. It's fun to laugh about rotting frogs and lunch at the pigpen, but God doesn't want *us* to be gross. Part of being a godly man is keeping your armpits clean, your undergarments fresh, your fingers out of your nose, your table manners decent, and your conversation clean. It's also a good way to keep friends. And friends are cool.

Gross-Cordance

For folks who like facts and figures, here is a collection of bizarre totals and totally nasty numbers straight from the Scriptures.

The number of times the Bible talks about vomit is thirteen. Even more gross, 2 Peter 2:22 talks about dogs vomiting, then slurping their barf up again. Nasty times two!

Did you know the Bible lists ninety-four specific people who are killed? And that's not including the people killed in battles or in unspecified numbers. Then it'd be in the hundreds of thousands!

Watch your step—the Bible mentions dung or excrement on fourteen occasions! Phew-weee!

Pigs usually get pretty bad press in the Bible—at least they do in the twenty-one times they're mentioned.

The number of kings and queens in the Bible who were assassinated hits double digits at ten, but that was enough to keep 'em from sitting too easily on the throne!
Including the huge battle between God's army and the forces of evil at the end of time, there are 109 accounts in the Bible of armies going into battle.

Most killed at once? In one battle against rebellious King Ahaz of Judah, the Israelites killed a whopping 120,000 soldiers—in *one* day (2 Chronicles 28:6).
Frogs are cool, unless they're piled in dead, stinking heaps after a plague. All told, frogs leap into the Bible fourteen times.

There's blood everywhere in the Bible! It's mentioned enough times to read about it once a day for a year and three months (give or take a drop or so)! Speaking of blood, did you know that the Bible talks about dogs lapping up human blood? (See 1 Kings 22:37–38.)

A jackal's eerie laughing howl can make your blood run cold! The Bible refers to jackals nineteen times, usually with the bone-chilling phrase, "A haunt of jackals," meaning a destroyed city where only jackals live.

The record number of bratty boys mauled by bears at one time still stands at forty-two. Of course, there were two bears involved (2 Kings 2:24). And the record hasn't been broken because no gangs of kids are particularly eager to break this record.

It's a good thing that God says so often, "Don't be afraid," because there are 456 times where the Bible talks about people being afraid.

Seven is the number of lion-related attacks mentioned in Scripture—it's just enough to make you think twice about making fun of that lazy, old, fat one at your local zoo.

The Bible mentions grasshoppers and locusts thirty-seven different times, and ten of those times we're talking *millions* of 'em at once in swarms and plagues!

Serpents and snakes slither sneakily into the Scriptures fifty-six times.

Imagine being a vulture, circling overhead, waiting for your dinner to die! These disgusting scavengers make it into the Bible eight times. Owls have them totally beat! Owls are mentioned twenty-two times, with *groups* of owls mentioned another five times!

Nakedness makes a strong showing in the Bible, with four dozen different mentions. Breezy!

Avoiding getting killed was a favorite. In the Bible, people ran for their lives a total of 126 times.

Leprosy, boils, and sores are painfully recorded in Scripture on fifty-one occasions. Ouch!

CAREFUL—THOSE THINGS ARE SHARP!

Apparently the memo on camping equipment safety never made it to Jael's tent because she went right to the top of the list when she impaled Sisera's head with a tent peg (Judges 4:21). Ah! Here it is: Top Five Things *Not* to Do with Tent Pegs: (5) Eat Chinese food; (4) Sew socks; (3) Pick your nose; (2) Pick someone else's nose; (1) Drive one through someone's head into the ground.

WHAT DO YOU MEAN, "A GIRL DROPPED THAT MILLSTONE"?

The truly amazing thing about Abimelech's death wasn't that a woman dropped a millstone from a tower and that the talented guy caught it with his head. Nope—the millstone didn't *kill* him. The most incredible thing is that he was still able to talk and tell his armor-bearer to finish the job (Judges 9:52–54). Apparently he didn't want anyone to think that a woman had killed him. He probably was a little insecure about his manliness.

POOR ELI—THAT LAST STEP WAS A DOOZY

Old man Eli led Israel for forty years and probably was looking forward to a nice, quiet retirement recalling Israel's victories and eating doughnuts. Instead this *very* heavy guy gets the *very* heavy news that the Philistines captured the ark of God. He's so shocked that he topples backwards off his chair, and so large that he breaks his neck and dies (1 Samuel 4:16–18). Bad news and too many doughnuts can be *really* bad news.

You Made Your Bed . . . Now Lie in It

Evil Haman was determined to destroy the Jews in Persia. He plotted and planned and even built a gallows seventy-five feet high for a Jew named Mordecai. (Seventy-five feet? That is *definitely* overkill.) But Mordecai's cousin Esther foiled Haman's plan, and Haman himself died on his own humongous invention (Esther 7:9–10). This contraption of death might have been a huge pointy pole that Haman was impaled on.

Head on a Platter

Drunk King Herod lost his head and promised his stepdaughter, Salome, anything she wanted—up to half of his kingdom. She *could've* asked for all the cities of Galilee! No? Or how about all the palaces in Perea? What's she *asked* for was the head of John the Baptist delivered to her on a platter! (Mark 6:21–28) It's a shame that Herod lost his head, because it cost John his head permanently.

Another Horrid Herod Dies!

Herod the Great's grandson (*another* horrid Herod) lived a nasty life and died a nasty death—he was literally eaten alive by worms

(Acts 12:23)! These probably were roundworms that fed on fluids in his intestines and eventually killed him.

BLOOD UP TO THE HORSES' BRIDLES

Part of John's vision in the Revelation was a massive bloodbath that hasn't happened yet, but will in the future when the wicked are dumped like grapes into the "winepress" of God's anger and *stomped* (Revelation 14:20). There will be so many killed that the blood will slosh as high as a horse's bridle—five feet deep—for almost one hundred eighty miles! Now, imagine all the dead *bodies* floating in all that blood! Major gross out!

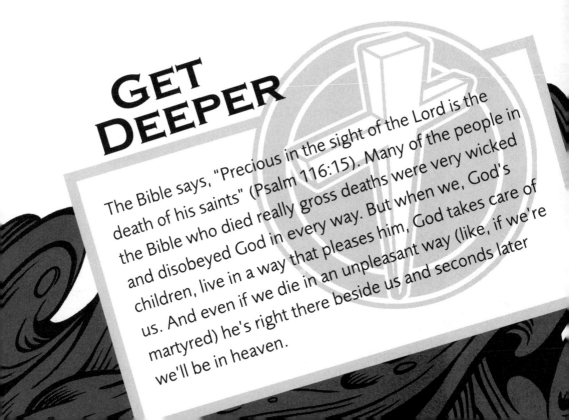

GET DEEPER

The Bible says, "Precious in the sight of the Lord is the death of his saints" (Psalm 116:15). Many of the people in the Bible who died really gross deaths were very wicked and disobeyed God in every way. But when we, God's children, live in a way that pleases him, God takes care of us. And even if we die in an unpleasant way (like, if we're martyred) he's right there beside us and seconds later we'll be in heaven.

JUST ABOUT DIED LAUGHING

Abraham and Sarah were really old (100 and 90, respectively) when God told them that they were going to have a baby. The idea sort of tickled them. In fact, Abraham laughed so hard that he *fell down* laughing (Genesis 17:15–17). Falling down probably was more dangerous for a guy his age than having a kid. And Sarah caught the chuckles too (Genesis 18:12–15). So a year later when their son was born, they named him Isaac, which means "laughter" (Genesis 21:1–6).

GOD SITS IN HEAVEN, LAUGHING

Psalms 2:4 and 37:13 paint an interesting picture of God: He's laughing! What's he laughing at? Picture all the nations and people of the world that have decided God doesn't exist, or that he's "dead," or on vacation. They talk real big and real loud, but God just kicks back on his throne in heaven, laughing at their foolishness.

Thousands of years ago in Egypt, cats were worshiped as gods. As you can see by their attitude, cats have never forgotten this.

After Adam and Eve were kicked out of the Garden of Eden, Adam was out walking with his sons Cain and Abel. When they passed by the ruins of the Garden, Cain asked, "What's that?" Adam answered, "That's where your mom and I ate ourselves out of house and home."

A very Bible-minded mother had *two* sets of twins (all boys) and one set of triplets (again, all boys). She called the twins First and Second Samuel, and First and Second Peter. The triplets were named First, Second, and Third John. (Just joking.)

GET COOLER

God invented humor and laughter, and probably made up the first joke. A good sense of humor is a great thing to have. Being funny—genuinely funny, not just goofy or sarcastic—is something we can work on and develop. And it's definitely something we can control. We *need* to! The Bible says that we should stay away from foolish and sinful joking (Ephesians 5:4). God wants us to laugh out loud, enjoy a good joke, and develop a good, clean sense of humor.

MORE WEIRD TRIVIA

Q: Abdon had forty sons and thirty grandsons who rode on seventy donkeys. True or false?

A: True. (Judges 12:13–14)

Q: Ezekiel had to eat nothing but rats and seaweed for three years. True or false?

A: False.

Q: When blessing some children, Jesus told them they should eat their vegetables. True or false?

A: False.

Q: People in Israel sometimes tore their clothes and put dust on their heads when they were really upset. True or false?

A: True. (2 Samuel 15:32)

Q: When some angels appeared to Abraham, he offered them curds to eat. True or false?

A: True. (Genesis 18:8)

Q: The book of Zacchaeus is the shortest book in the Old Testament. True or false?

A: False. There is no book of Zacchaeus in the Bible.

Q: Jesus told a story about a man who had dogs licking his sores. True or false?

A: True. (Luke 16:19–21)

Q: Although they had lots of house cats as pets in Egypt, they're mentioned in the Bible only three times. True or false?

A: False. They're not mentioned at all.

Q: Moses built the ark for his family and the animals out of gopher wood.

A: False. Noah built the ark.

OUTRAGEOUS LIES & EXCUSES

HOW MANY FINGERS AM I HOLDING UP, DAD?

Jacob tricked his father, Isaac, into giving him his brother's blessing by pretending to be Esau. He pulled it off because dear ol' Dad was practically blind (Genesis 27:1, 15–23). "Esau, my son, is that you?" "Um, y-yes (ahem), I mean, *yes,* Father! It is I, Esau, your hairy son. No smooth-skinned, weenie-boy Jacob here!" "You certainly *smell* like Esau, my son." "Yes, I am very . . . *manly* smelling." "Come receive my blessing, my son." "Great! Um, Father, I'm over here."

AARON AND THE GOLDEN BALONEY

Moses comes down from Mount Sinai with the Ten Commandments and—can you *believe* it—here is his brother Aaron leading the people in worshiping a golden calf! Aaron had *made* the idol, but when Moses shouts, "Where did this calf come from?" Aaron mumbles, "The people gave me the gold, and I threw it into the fire, and out came this calf!" (Exodus 32:22–24). "Oh, sure! Right, Aaron! Just like *that*? You sure the tooth fairy didn't make it out of gold fillings?" Moses probably wanted to bust the Ten Commandments over Aaron's head.

MOLDY BREAD, WORN OUT SHOES

Joshua and the Israelites attacked Canaan, wiping people out like Windex. The Gibeonites rode out in rags to meet the Israelites. Wearing worn-out shoes and bringing moldy bread, the Gibeonites pretended they were from a faraway country. "Oh, we're so poor—we'd offer you some bread but it's all blue and *gnarly*. Oh, I've got to get this *pebble* out of my hole-y shoe!" (Joshua 9:3–15). Since God hadn't told the Israelites to attack faraway nations, they made a treaty with the tricky Gibeonites. For an encore, you almost wonder why the Gibeonites didn't try to sell Joshua the Brooklyn Bridge!

I Did What You Said . . .

King Saul kept screwing up and making excuses for not obeying God. Like when he was supposed to wipe out the Amalekites completely, but didn't. Samuel called him on it, but Saul made a lame excuse. "But, I *did* what God told me to do! You said, 'No captives,' and hey, I only took the *king* as a captive. You told me, "No taking plunder,' so I just kept their *best* stuff—you know, for *God* and all that" (1 Samuel 15:1–3, 13–21). (What? Did he think that Samuel was stupid?) Samuel shook his head. "Yeah, you did every single thing right—except for every single thing you did."

Ananias and Sapphira Drop Dead

Ananias and Sapphira sold some land and kept some of the cash for themselves. No problem there. But then they lied, "We're flat broke.

Boo-hoo. We gave *every* single bit of the money to the church." Peter said, "What's the deal? You could've done whatever you wanted with your land or money but, like, why try to trick God?" Pete might as well have said, "Drop dead," because that's just what Ananias did. And it's exactly what Sapphira did three hours later when Peter asked her the same question (Acts 5:1–10). Conning people is bad enough but trying to lie to or trick God is insane.

GET COOLER

The truth is always its own best defense. In other words, if you always tell the truth, you never have to try to remember what lie you told in order to make everything line up. When you make a commitment to always tell the truth, people begin to trust what you say, and therefore, trust you. That opens up lots of possibilities and opportunities in life. When you lie, people learn not to trust you, and your opportunities and possibilities dry up.

HALL OF FAME

HALL OF FAME—ELISHA

After Elijah was taken to heaven in a whirlwind, his sidekick, Elisha, became the new prophet on the block. Let's have a look at just a few of the incredible miracles performed by this wild and wooly man of God.

When a pack of young toughs called him a "bald-head," Elisha called down a curse, and two bears came out of the woods and mowed down forty-two of the wise guys (2 Kings 2:23–24). Important lesson number one: Don't mock people. Important lesson number two: Bald prophets are very sensitive, so be nice.

Another time Elisha thought, *It's gotta be the staff!* He sent a servant with his wooden staff to try to raise a dead boy, but the staff didn't do diddly. Then Elisha himself went, and he prayed and raised the boy from death (2 Kings 4:29–35). After that, Elisha knew that he could never send the staff to do the boss's work. Once Elisha's servant cooked up a pot of stew for a group of prophets. Some guy who wasn't exactly a gourd expert sliced a poisonous gourd into the pot. They're in the middle of a famine, everybody's hungry, dinner's been poisoned, and they're all staring at the Gourd Guy. Elisha said, "Would you guys chill?" He had them throw some flour in, and the stew was fine (2 Kings 4:39–41). (How'd he do *that*?) Another time Elisha threw some salt in undrinkable water, and after that the water was fine (2 Kings 2:19–22).

Another time, Elisha healed a rich officer, Naaman of leprosy, but when Naaman tried to repay him with riches, Elisha refused. Elisha's servant Gehazi did not. He took Naaman's gifts and then tried to hide them from Elisha. Trying to hide stuff from a prophet of God—*that's* bright! "So, where have you been, Gehazi?" "What? Me? I didn't go anywhere. How about some nice lemonade?" "Uh-huh, right. You took Naaman's gifts, but you forgot one of his things—his leprosy. Now it's yours too." (2 Kings 5:1–27)

One day while Elisha and his servant were in the city of Dothan, the Assyrians surrounded the city.

"We're surrounded!" Elisha's servant saw only the humongous enemy army around them. Oh yeah? God opened his eyes so that he could see the surrounding hills, which were *filled* with the fiery chariots and horses of the army of God (2 Kings 6:15–17). "*Now* who's surrounded?"

After Elisha died, some Israelites were burying a guy when they heard some bandits coming. They panicked and dumped the corpse in a nearby tomb. The tomb happened to be where Elisha was buried, and when the body flopped down onto Elisha's bones, the dead man came back to life again. "Hey, Jacob, I think we probably should've buried Zeb better." "Why do you say that?" "Because here he comes down the road" (2 Kings 13:21)!

Talking to the Dead Is a Dead End

The prophet Isaiah warned against seeking the advice of mediums—people who talk to the dead (Isaiah 8:19). Why talk to dead people to find out what only the living God knows, right? Of course, that hasn't stopped people today from attending séances and trying to talk to Grandma to find out what the secret ingredient was in her special meatloaf. Truth is there are just some things we're not supposed to know, and talking to the dead is definitely a dead issue. Don't mess with it!

Confused? Have You Talked to Your Liver?

The mighty king of Babylon had three ways he used to tell the future. First, he would "shake the arrows," which was sort of like drawing straws. Next, he would consult an idol to see if some spirit would guide him. Finally, he would have his priests check out the liver of a sacrificed animal to see if its shape and size would give him direction (Ezekiel 21:21). Oh, yeah, that's just *great*, king! Play pickup sticks, talk to chunks of stone, and "read" the daily liver. But prayer? No—that's too *weird*!

DISTANT BALLS OF GAS

Those Babylonian kings had lousy advisers. Whenever the king had a serious problem, the astrologers failed to provide a solution (Daniel 2:10, 2:27, and 5:7). But they were great at providing excuses: "Oh, wow, man, that's a tough one! Like, only the gods know the answer to that one, your royal royalness. And they're, like, totally out of cellular range. Sorry, king-dude." What did the king expect? That stars—distant balls of burning gas millions of light-years away—are going to shell out all the answers? *Riiight.*

Worshiping Firewood and Doorstops

It's pretty amazing to think that people actually worshiped objects made of wood and stone (Deuteronomy 4:28, Ezekiel 20:32, and Daniel 5:4 are just a few examples). Why worship something that's been created when you could worship the One who created it? Almighty God, maker of heaven and earth—or some little ugly dude chipped out of driftwood with big, googly eyes and a crooked nose. Get real! What kind of god doubles as kindling or a paperweight?

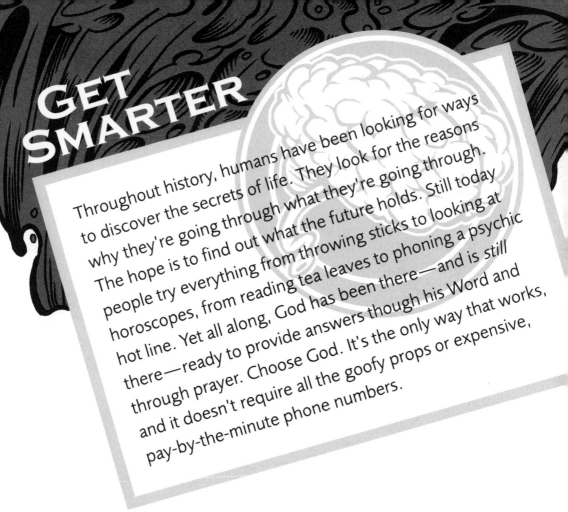

GET SMARTER

Throughout history, humans have been looking for ways to discover the secrets of life. They look for the reasons why they're going through what they're going through. The hope is to find out what the future holds. Still today people try everything from throwing sticks to looking at horoscopes, from reading tea leaves to phoning a psychic hot line. Yet all along, God has been there—and is *still* there—ready to provide answers though his Word and through prayer. Choose God. It's the only way that works, and it doesn't require all the goofy props or expensive, pay-by-the-minute phone numbers.

BUGS & INSECTS

Bugs and insects were created on the sixth day of Creation with the "creatures that move along the ground" (Genesis 1:24).

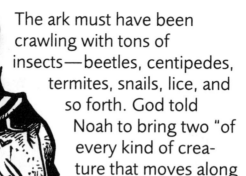

The ark must have been crawling with tons of insects—beetles, centipedes, termites, snails, lice, and so forth. God told Noah to bring two "of every kind of creature that moves along the ground" (Genesis 6:20).

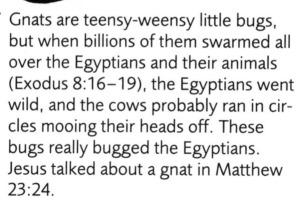

Gnats are teensy-weensy little bugs, but when billions of them swarmed all over the Egyptians and their animals (Exodus 8:16–19), the Egyptians went wild, and the cows probably ran in circles mooing their heads off. These bugs really bugged the Egyptians. Jesus talked about a gnat in Matthew 23:24.

One of the plagues that God sent upon the Egyptians was filthy flies (Exodus 8:20–24). Gazillions of them! "Dense swarms of flies poured into Pharaoh's palace . . . and throughout Egypt the land was ruined by flies" (verse 24).

Here comes insect plague number three—the locust plague! (Exodus 10:1–19). Locusts are like grasshoppers, only bigger, "They invaded all Egypt . . . . They covered all the ground until it was black" (verses 14–15). Imagine walking along. Crunch, crunch, crunch, crunch. Part of that crunching sound was locusts eating everything in sight.

Here's a list of insects that the Jewish people could eat: "All flying insects that walk on all fours are to be detestable to you. There are, however, some winged creatures that walk on all fours that you may eat . . . you may eat any kind of locust, katydid, cricket or grasshopper" (Leviticus 11:20–22).

When King Saul was hunting David in the mountains, David compared himself to a flea (1 Samuel 24:14; 26:20). He was saying,

"I'm such a little nuthin'. Why are you bothering to chase me?"

King David must have been in some pretty wild battles. In Psalm 118:12 he said about his enemies: "They swarmed around me like bees."

Wanna read about spiders' webs? Take a look at Job 8:14 and Isaiah 59:5.

Ants are so hardworking! They just never stop moving! Even King Solomon was amazed by those formidable little *Formicidae*. (See Proverbs 6:6; 30:25.)

Leeches look like slugs, but have suckers on the ends of their bodies to suck blood. *Your* blood. Proverbs 30:15 talks about a leech with two daughters.

The "worm" that chewed the vine that Jonah sat under was a *Lepidopterous* larva with one *huge* appetite (Jonah 4:7).

Both Job and Jesus talked about the moths eating clothes (Job 13:28; Matthew 6:19).

When Job talked about "worms" covering dead bodies, he was talking about fly maggots (Job 21:26).

Herod was eaten alive by worms (Acts 12:23). Not a nice way to go.

TOTALLY MORONIC FIGHTS— PART ONE: PHARAOH TAKES ON GOD

From the moment Pharaoh decided to ignore the God of Israel (Exodus 5:2), he made his own life and the life of every Egyptian harder. He figured, "The Hebrew slaves have a god? Since they're my slaves, I guess I must be greater and more powerful than he is." Ten plagues later, he was whistling a different tune.

TOTALLY MORONIC FIGHTS— PART TWO: PHARAOH TAKES ON THE RED SEA

Shortly after the Hebrews left, it was as if someone splashed Pharaoh with cold water—"Wait a minute! We let the Hebrews *go*? Are we nuts? Who's gonna do the work around here? Let's go after them!" Pharaoh took his entire army and chased the Israelites to the Red Sea. When God parted the waters and Moses scooted his people through, Pharaoh (get this!) actually ordered his men in after them (Exodus 14:5–28). Then the sea closed back in, drowning his entire army. *Think* about it: Here's God holding the sea apart and a guy who boasts that he's God's enemy walks *into* the sea! Duh!

GOD HEARS EVERYTHING

God came down in a pillar of cloud and busted Miriam, Moses' sister, and Aaron for saying some pretty critical things about his guy Moses. When the cloud lifted, Miriam was white with leprosy. She had to leave the camp and sit out on a rock for seven days (major time out!) until God healed her (Numbers 12:1–15).

KORAH REBELS THEN LOSES GROUND

Korah got some buddies together and spoke out against Moses (apparently choosing to ignore the whole Miriam episode). Moses just left the situation up to God. "If God didn't send me, you'll die a natural death. If he did send me, the earth will swallow you whole . . . right about . . . *now*" (Numbers 16:28–33). Since you know that God sent Moses, you can imagine the fate of Korah and Co. "And lo, the earth burped a mighty belch . . ."

ACHIN' ACHAN

Achan tried to bury some stolen stuff under his tent—silver and gold and a nice robe he took after Jericho fell. Instead of keeping God's *command* to destroy everything from Jericho, he *kept* the stuff. Whoops! When the truth was revealed, Achan had to 'fess up, and then he got stoned to death (Joshua 7:19–26). That was one expensive bathrobe!

WORLD'S SMARTEST MAN DUMBS OUT

Solomon had a reputation as the world's wisest man. So it's a bit of a mystery why the world's wisest man acted like such a dummy and started worshiping idols (1 Kings 11:4–7). That's right—he chose paperweights and firewood over God! And he did it just to make some of his seven hundred idol-worshiping wives happy. False gods? Seven hundred wives? Most paperweights are smarter than that!

AND HERE'S WHERE WE KEEP THE EXTRA KEY. . .

Hezekiah had been blessed by God and healed of a dangerous illness, but he let it go to his head (2 Chronicles 32:24–25) and did some pretty boneheaded things. He wanted to impress some ambassadors from Babylon, so he showed them all of Judah's treasure, weapons, and armor. Talk about giving your playbook to the other team! Nice move, coach! When Babylon rolled into town and crushed Judah

Q: Which book in the Bible is all about math?

A: Numbers.

years later, they had a good idea of the plunder they'd be taking home with them (2 Kings 20:12–17).

HAMAN PLOTS AGAINST THE KING'S WIFE

When Haman plotted to kill all the Jews in Persia, he was *clueless* that the king had married a Jewess named Esther. Queen Esther told the king of the threat to her and her people (Esther 7:3–6), and the king was all, "Who would dare do such a thing?" "Well," she said, "His name starts with an H, ends with an N, and rhymes with Hey-man." You better believe Haman was sweating bullets at that point!

IT SOUNDS BETTER WHEN YOU'RE NOT THE MAIN COURSE

A bunch of jealous nobles decided to trick the king into dumping Daniel. Plan works and plunk, Daniel is dropped into a den of hungry lions. Of course, God was with Daniel the whole time, and Dan was scratching them kitties under their chinny-chin-chins by the next morning. Naturally, they were *still hungry*, so they were pretty pleased when the king pulled Daniel out and chucked all the plotting nobles into the den instead (Daniel 6:3–24).

YOU JUST CAN'T BUY THAT IN STORES

Some things aren't for sale. Simon the sorcerer found this out when he tried to buy the power of the Holy Spirit so that he could heal and baptize people. Peter told him off. "May your money perish with you! What? You think the Holy Spirit of God is for sale? Get a *clue*, man!" All of a sudden Simon does some major backpedaling and begs Peter to pray for him (Acts 8:9–24). Apparently the "perish" part bothered him a little.

GET SMARTER

God is everywhere, knows everything, and can do anything. Yet, sometimes we get the idea that he doesn't care what we do. When we're tempted to do the wrong thing and think, It's gonna be OK. I won't get in trouble. Watch out! Galatians 6:7 says that God is not mocked. What we do and say does matter. We will reap what we sow. We're either planting good seed or we're planting bad seed. Yes, God will forgive us if we sin, then repent, but he's not going to dig up the seeds. The seeds will still grow. We need to do things God's way and plant good seeds.

BIBLE RECORDS

LONGEST LIVING GUY: METHUSELAH

Methuselah lived to be 969 years old (Genesis 5:27). Imagine what his last birthday cake must've looked like! They probably just lit a bonfire and threw the cake in it!

SINGLE WORST DAY, EVER: JOB

The worst single day anyone has ever had was when Job lost everything in a matter of hours. One after another, messengers dropped by to let Job know that he had lost all of his livestock, servants, and, worst of all, his ten children. His wife told him to curse God and die (Job 1:13–21; 2:9). When the day started, Job had it all; when it was over, he had nothing, *nada*, zippo, zilch—except God. And it turned out that God was more than enough.

QUICKEST DEMOLITION: JERICHO

The city of Jericho was famous for the high walls that protected it. There was no way that Joshua and the Israelites were going to get in on their own, so God told them to tromp around the city for a week, blow their trumpets, shout, and watch the walls fall down (Joshua 6:1–

20). Sounds wacky, but it worked. Josh and company two-stepped around the walls for a week, made some noise, and God brought in the invisible wrecking ball. Presto-whammo, Jericho got slammo'd!

WORST NAME GOING: NABAL

In Bible times, names always had a literal meaning that was supposed to describe that person's character and personality. So you can imagine what kind of a person Nabal was. His name meant "fool." Unfortunately, he lived up to it (or down to it) when he treated David rudely (1 Samuel 25:2–38).

RICHEST GUY IN BIBLE TIMES: SOLOMON

God asked Solomon what gift he wanted, and Solomon asked for the brains to tell right from wrong and to rule God's people. God was so pleased that he made Sol the richest king alive (1 Kings 3:8–13).

FASTEST GUY IN THE BIBLE: ELIJAH

God gave Elijah the ability to outrace a chariot and a thunderstorm (1 Kings 18:45–46). Elijah ran ahead of Ahab's chariot for the entire six miles from Mount Carmel to Jezreel. Now, a chariot could travel upwards of twenty miles an hour, which means that Elijah was *moving*—about a mile every three minutes!

WILDEST CHARIOT DRIVER ON RECORD: JEHU

Jehu took chariot racing to the next level, burning up the road between Ramoth Gilead and Jezreel in order to take over the throne. Jehu had a reputation for driving like a madman (2 Kings 9:16–20). Can you imagine what he'd be like if he was a kid today and owned a skateboard? Whoa!

TWO YOUNGEST KINGS: JOASH & JOSIAH

You know that the Israelites were living in interesting times when they had to put second-graders on the throne. Joash became king when he was seven (2 Kings 11:21), and Josiah took the throne when he was eight (2 Kings 22:1)! Joash got off to a good start before his chief adviser died, and the other young king, Josiah, did a great job of getting the people's minds back on God. Kids rule!

PROPHET WHO OUT-CRIED ALL OTHER PROPHETS: JEREMIAH

Being one of God's prophets was a really tough job, but Jeremiah won hands down for most tears per prophecy. He was known as the "weeping prophet" because he could see all the bad stuff coming, but no matter how much he warned, people just wouldn't listen up (Jeremiah 9:1; Lamentations 1:1–2). Maybe that's where the expression Town Crier came from.

STRANGEST EATING HABITS: JOHN THE BAPTIST

You'd probably expect a prophet—those wild and wacky guys—to have a pretty strange diet. John the Baptist, however, takes the cake (not literally)—he chowed down on locusts and wild honey (Matthew 3:4). Locusts are like grasshoppers, only bigger and crunchier, and he probably had to battle wild bees for the honey. They didn't have McDavid's back then.

HEY, YOU'VE FINALLY REACHED THE END OF THE BOOK!

Maybe it was so much fun that you were hoping it would never end? Don't worry, there are other books in this series! Yep! Even more books full of more bizarre Bible stories! Hopefully we've made you laugh, grossed you out more than just a little, and made you realize just how extremely interesting God's Word is.

No denying it: the Bible is full of strange stuff: vomit-slurping dogs, fish that swallow people—and their money—strange creatures and, oh, yes . . . very strange people. Some of the stories we've read were so wild, you can almost imagine hilarious home videos of these people on some TV show. And just like the people in those videos, the people in the Bible were ordinary, everyday folks to whom some very unusual things happened.

That's right! These were real things that happened to real people. (OK, OK, apart from the seven-headed dragons and stuff.) This shows that God isn't just involved in your prayer life. He doesn't just sort of drop by for a few moments when you kneel down to pray, but he's with you every minute of every day in every single thing you think, say, and do. God is always at work in your life, trying to make you stronger, deeper, cooler, and smarter, just like he was with Jesus when Jesus was a kid (Luke 2:52).

Think of some of the things that have happened to you: maybe they seemed funny, gross, or weird at the time, but you learned a lesson from them. How about your most embarrassing moment? Some weird sickness? A crazy prayer that God answered? A joke? Something zany you've read in this book? Think of things that taught you something spiritual and changed you for the better. Bingo! That's God at work in your life, making you smarter, cooler, deeper, and stronger.

2:52 Soul Gear™ Laptop fiction books—
Technological thrillers that will keep you on the edge of your seat...

Laptop 1: Reality Shift
They Changed the Future
Written by Christopher P. N. Maselli
Softcover 0-310-70338-7

Laptop 2: Double-Take
Things are Not What They Seem
Written by Christopher P. N. Maselli
Softcover 0-310-70339-5

Laptop 3: Explosive Secrets
*Not Everything Lost
Is Meant to Be Found*
Written by Christopher P. N. Maselli
Softcover 0-310-70340-9

Laptop 4: Power Play
Beware of Broken Promises
Written by Christopher P. N. Maselli
Softcover 0-310-70341-7

Zonderkidz.

The 2:52 Boys Bible–
the "ultimate *manual*" for boys!

The 2:52 Boys Bible, NIV
General Editor Rick Osborne

From the metal-looking cover to the cool features inside, *The 2:52 Boys Bible, NIV* is filled with tons of fun and interesting facts–yup, even gross ones, too!–that only a boy could appreciate. Based on Luke 2:52: "And Jesus grew in wisdom and stature, and in favor with God and men," this Bible will help boys ages 8-12 become more like Jesus mentally, physically, spiritually, and socially–Smarter, Stronger, Deeper, and Cooler!

Hardcover 0-310-70320-4
Softcover 0-310-70552-5

Zonder**kidz**.

This great CD holder for young boys has a rubber 2:52 Soul Gear™ logo patch stitched onto cool nylon material. This cover will look great with the newly released 2:52 Soul Gear™ products. The interior has 12 sleeves to hold 24 favorite CDs.

$9.99 ($15.50 Cdn)

ISBN: 0-310-99033-5
UPC: 025986990336

This cool book and Bible Cover for young boys will look great with the newly released 2:52 Soul Gear™ products. It features a rubber 2:52 logo patch stitched down onto microfiber material. The zipper pull is black with 2:52 embroidered in gray. The interior has pen/pencil holders.

$14.99 ($22.50 Cdn) each

Large	ISBN: 0-310-98824-1
	UPC: 025986988241
Med	ISBN: 0-310-98823-3
	UPC: 025986988234

inspirio
The gift group of Zondervan

We want to hear from you. Please send your comments about this book to us in care of the address below. Thank you.

Zonder**kidz**®

Grand Rapids, MI 49530
www.zonderkidz.com